Mel Bay Presents

Tex-Mex Conjunto Classics for Accordion

Transcribed and Arranged by Gary Dahl

For Diatonic or Piano Accordion

Contents

Visit us on the Web at www.melbay.com — E-mail us at email@melbay.com

Ay Te Dejo En San Antonio

Flaco Jiménez

4

Connie

Paulino Bernal

Cuando Se Pierde La Madre

Lydia Mendoza

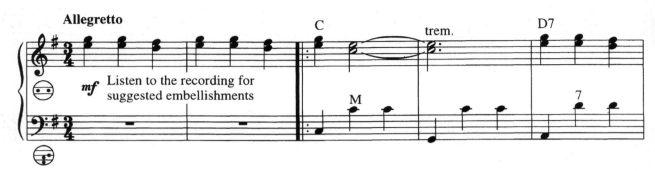

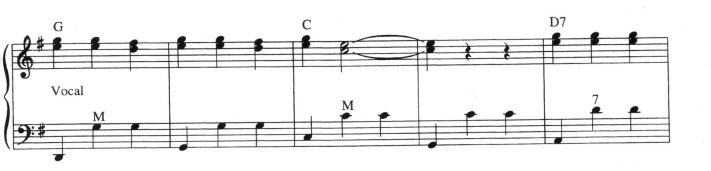

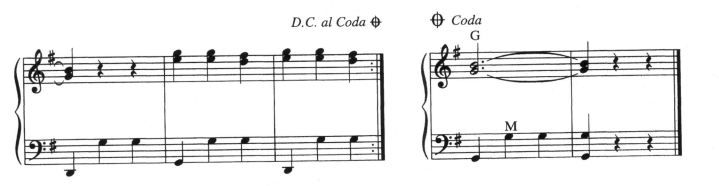

Cada Vez Que Cae La Tarde

Santiago Jimenez Jr.

13

Zulema

Don Santiago Jiménez

D.C. al Coda ⊕   ⊕ *Coda*

Alejamiento Y Regreso

Los Pavos Reales

D.S. %̸ al Coda ⊕   ⊕ *Coda*

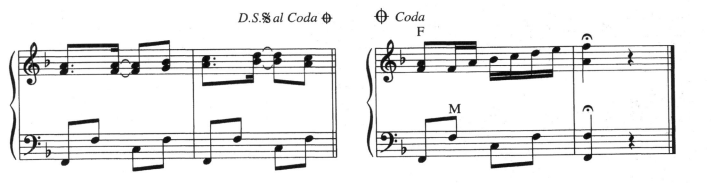

Atotonilco

Tony De La Rosa

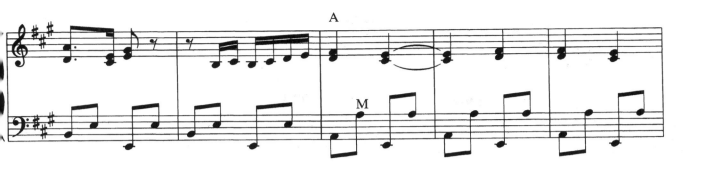

El Canoero

Valerio Longoria

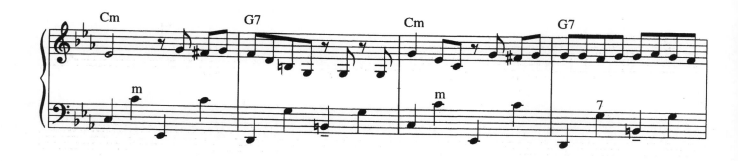

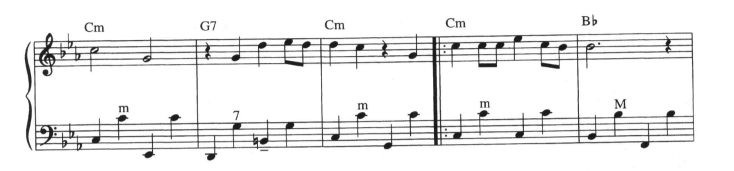

27

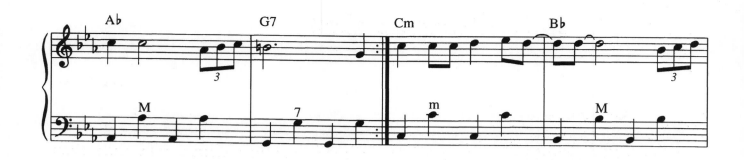

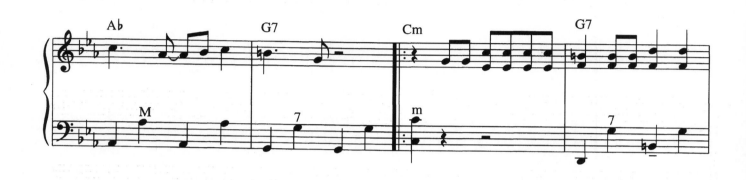

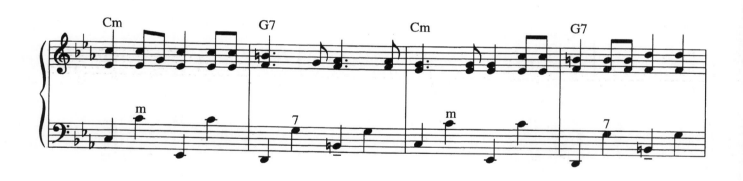

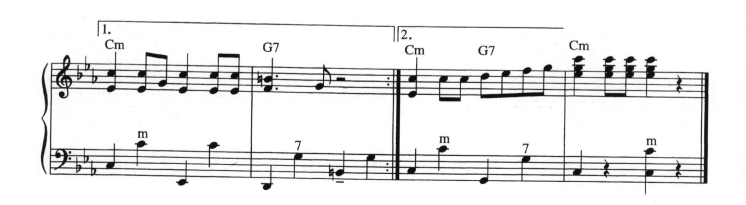

Hazme Caso

Steve Jordan

Corrido de César Chávez

Los Pingüinos Del Norte

Pasos Cortos

Juan Lopez

No Me Estorbes

Fred Zimmerle &
Trio San Antonio

Luzita

Narciso Martinez

El Mexicano-Americano

Los Cenzontles

Negra Traición

Flaco Jiménez

About the Author

Gary Dahl is an accordionist, composer, arranger, recording artist and educator residing in Puyallup, Washington. He is certified by the American Accordionist's Association and received a BA degree from the University of Washington with a minor in music theory and harmony. Mr. Dahl's students have been consistent winners in national/state competitions and many have achieved professional status. The Gary Dahl Trio plus vocalist performed regularly at private clubs, hotels, and lounges. Today Gary Dahl is heard as a soloist for exclusive private functions and is busy writing and recording.

Printed in Great
Britain
by Amazon